Good Ideas!

By Leslie A. Rotsky

Scott Foresman
is an imprint of

Glenview, Illinois • Boston, Massachusetts • Chandler, Arizona •
Upper Saddle River, New Jersey

Photographs

Every effort has been made to secure permission and provide appropriate credit for photographic material. The publisher deeply regrets any omission and pledges to correct errors called to its attention in subsequent editions.

Unless otherwise acknowledged, all photographs are the property of Pearson Education, Inc.

Photo locators denoted as follows: Top (T), Center (C), Bottom (B), Left (L), Right (R), Background (Bkgd)

Opener: ©FoodCollection/SuperStock; **1** ©Greg Elms/StockFood Creative/Getty Images; **3** ©Blend Images/Getty Images; **4** ©FoodCollection/SuperStock; **5** Jupiter Images; **6** ©Greg Elms/StockFood Creative/Getty Images; **7** FoodCollection/SuperStock; **8** ©eStock Photo/Alamy Images.

ISBN 13: 978-0-328-46344-2
ISBN 10:   0-328-46344-2

The hot dog is good.
A bun helps me eat it.

The meat is good.

A tortilla helps me eat it.

The ice cream is good.
A cone helps me eat it.

The cheese is good.

Bread helps me eat it.

The salsa is good.
Chips help me eat it.

The yogurt is good.

A spoon helps me eat it!